MW00596561

AT HOME WITHIN

WITHIN

A Little Book of
Self-Care Wisdom

Meredith Gaston

Hardie Grant

BOOKS

DEAREST YOU,

This is a little book about cultivating the art of self-care
and nurturing a joyous, comforting sense of 'home' within
yourself. Relax and enjoy this book as you explore pathways
to peace, balance and contentment in daily life. Learn to
nurture your inner world with kindness and compassion,
and feel encouraged as you fall more deeply in love with
yourself and your life each step of the way.

The ideas and inspirations that grace these pages will
assist you to create profoundly positive change within.
As you change, the world around you will transform too,
delighting and guiding you.

No matter what state of heart this book finds you
experiencing at this very moment, please know that
you have everything you need to proceed.

May you feel treasured and supported at every turn.

Love, Meredith X

CONTENTS

ENJOYING THIS BOOK

This little book is composed of ten inspirational chapters on self-care, a practice that can help us feel more at home within ourselves each and every day. Feeling at home within involves caring for ourselves in loving, thoughtful and joyous ways. It also involves noticing, honouring and meeting our unique needs in daily life. When we meet our own needs and nourish ourselves generously, we bring so much more to ourselves, each other and the world.

Essential to self-care is the nurturing of a personalised foundation of wellbeing, which supports us at every turn. Our wellbeing encompasses the thoughts we choose to think, the words we speak and the actions we take moment to moment. Wellbeing is so fulsome and integrative that it is not just a part of life but a way of life. Nurturing our wellbeing touches all parts of our aliveness – our vitality and mindfulness, courage and vulnerability, remarkable uniqueness and heartfelt togetherness.

Life calls us to tend devotedly to ourselves so that we may participate fully in the richness and splendour of living. Each one of us can experience the compelling, creative and ever-changing adventure of life: a journey in which we are invited to be ourselves, create positive change, care for ourselves unconditionally and blossom in confidence, joy and peace.

PAUL KLEE • PAINTING MUSIC

BEYOND THE EASEL

Health at Home   1st EDITION   Jenkin Howman

ENERGY MEDICINE

Watercolour Bold & Free

While nurturing a loving foundation provides us with immense solace and inspiration, we are by no means in this life alone. Learning to soothe ourselves while also welcoming others' tenderness, guidance and care into our lives with discretion and gratitude is an art in itself.

Cultivating loving and supportive relationships grounded in mutual respect and thoughtfulness is essential self-care.

When we feel at home within ourselves we can enjoy life and each other, just as we are. We are able to nurture honest, uplifting connections with others in which our sense of integrity and self-esteem flourish. Together we can share our inspiration and motivation for life, encouraging each other to see that when we feel at home within ourselves, we may feel at home in our bonds with one another and the world around us too. Indeed, when at home within we are home wherever we are.

Please enjoy these self-care wisdoms, affirmations and little prayers. You may like to read this book from cover to cover or dip in and out of its pages at your whim. Please note that the word 'prayer' has been thoughtfully reclaimed from any conventional or specific context. I see prayers as emanations from our hearts: little conversations with the energy of life from which we spring and to which we return. The prayers in this book are expressions of commitment to ourselves: celebrations of gratitude for life and living. I encourage you to draw inspiration from these prayers, embellishing them and making them your own.

By virtue of our aliveness each one of us belongs at home within. Nestled within us at all times dwells the creative energy of life: our vitality and our consciousness. As human beings we are by nature living, breathing expressions of divine, all-encompassing creative energy. Despite what our thinking minds may tell us, we are never alone, lost or disconnected. Indeed, when we connect with our inner worlds we connect with the energy of life. And this is our true home.

Please remember that one positive thought, word or act can change your whole day, even your whole life.

Oftentimes we are the ones standing in our own way with outworn, self-limiting thoughts and beliefs. Liberating ourselves to love and celebrate ourselves through daily self-care is the greatest gift. It is a gift that we can share with others in each and every exchange, and that brings light to the world in more profound and magical ways than we could ever possibly imagine.

I encourage you to never underestimate the power of self-care and mindful living, and to have deep faith in your natural capacity for learning and growing in this mysterious, wonderful life.

CARING FOR OURSELVES

Each day we live we are gifted the chance to know
and care for ourselves more deeply and lovingly.
Our unique life experiences imbue us with wisdom,
and, with divine timing, lead us on tremendous
journeys of discovery within and beyond. Our
personal journeys are coloured by highs and
lows, great mysteries and serendipitous insights.
Sometimes our journeys seem familiar, while at other
times they involve courageous leaps of faith into
the unknown. Regardless of our individual natures
or circumstances, each one of us inevitably becomes
an explorer of our outer and inner worlds as long
as we live: creative voyagers on our paths of life.

To enjoy our lives to the fullest we require the solidity and comfort of a very special relationship: a relationship with ourselves. This is without a doubt the most important, challenging, transformative and sublime relationship we will ever know – the one most worthy of our generosity, time and care.

The once-in-a-lifetime bond that we create with ourselves is, at its best, an art form of unconditional tenderness and care. It is strengthened by respect and compassion and bolstered by our own intuition and self-awareness. When we prioritise and nurture our relationship with ourselves, we may truly know and trust ourselves as we travel through life. We may sustain ourselves with the refreshment of inspiration, the peace of gratitude, and the luminous comfort of our own love.

No matter where we may go or what life may bring, caring for ourselves with love means that we may always feel at home within, safe in the trusted comfort of our very own inner sanctuary. Indeed, we may return home within at any moment amid the vivid outer adventures of our daily lives. As a wondrous added benefit, by tending to our inner worlds the richness and beauty we cultivate within touches and elevates all parts of our outer world too. Indeed, as we love and care for our home within, we shape and enhance every aspect and moment of our lives.

Each and every one of us is capable and worthy of knowing deep fulfilment, harmony and joy through the practice of daily self-care. Self-care ranges from the subtlest gestures, such as intercepting a negative thought, to the simple bliss of an early night; from quality quiet time to the most grandiose gesture of self-celebration imaginable.

Self-care is always an option, and, like any art
in life, the more we practise and attend to it,
the more natural and effortless it becomes.

Anchored and supported by a feeling of peace within, we can trust ourselves to come back to centre more swiftly, in the face of life challenges both great and small. Over time, as we acclimatise to a more harmonious inner world, we can simply feel when we have strayed from balance, and lovingly support ourselves to return as nimbly as possible to peace.

Looking inward to truly know ourselves, trusting in the power of our own support and care, being kind towards ourselves during both smooth and trying times, while choosing unwavering self-compassion and courageous honesty: these are the heavenly recipes for cultivating a sense of homeliness within. Taking the time to enjoy our uniqueness and design our lives in closest keeping with our innermost needs and values is profoundly rewarding self-care.

To love ourselves is the beginning
of a life-long romance.

Oscar Wilde

Oscar Wilde reminds us that to love ourselves is the beginning of a lifelong romance. As we are our only lifelong companion we are very wise to make sure that we truly enjoy our own company; that we feel right at home within. When we are gentle and encouraging with ourselves, when we regain perspective through gratitude, lightness and loving vision, and when we put ourselves first without guilt, shame or fear, knowing that we truly do matter, we blossom.

As we blossom at home within we begin to see and know ourselves through the eyes of love. The love that grows within us inspires our personal expression of energy and shapes our lives. Indeed, the love we possess for ourselves and for life emanates from within us. Without words, this love nurtures and inspires others with whom we share our lives. Herein lies the great importance of self-care: a revolutionary, expansive and creative art of love.

AFFIRMATION

I choose to honour myself with
true love and care.

JOURNAL PROMPTS

When I think of self-care,
I visualise ...

Practising self-care is important
to me because ...

As I imagine myself blossoming through
love, this is what I see and feel ...

PRAYER

I am deeply grateful for my life
and for the endless chances I am
gifted to learn, grow and blossom.
I treat myself with love today, inviting
perspective and peace into every moment
with each new breath. I am thankful for
the precious gifts of joy and fulfilment I
sense when I care for myself. As I blossom
in my own love, I notice the world around
me echoing my joy.

AT HOME
WITHIN

Deep within each of us is a sublime private haven to which we may always retreat. A place where heaven and earth meet. This precious, blissful and timeless sanctuary is our true home. Indeed while we may 'move home' at times in our lives, our inner abode is our constant, lifelong place of belonging.

It is very important that we feel cosy at home within: that we can rest, relax, feel soothed and uplifted whenever we please. By nurturing a sense of heaven within us, we feel much better equipped to face any and every situation in our outer worlds. We can always know that true peace, comfort and joy are only ever a heartbeat away: not somewhere 'out there' to be found but here, at home within.

Breathe deeply in and slowly out as you gently visualise a home within your heart, imagining various little rooms to inhabit, explore and enjoy. You might like to place your hand upon your heart now as you sink deeper into your own presence. Notice that, just like any home, your home within requires your love, time and care to become a comfortable and beautiful place to be. You might visualise lovely furnishings for your inner home as you pursue connection and beauty in daily life. Let new light and air in with your deep, mindful breaths, one by one. Grow an enchanting garden with your generous self-talk and positive thoughts, moment to moment. Renovate and redecorate when necessary through courageous journeys of transformation.

With each nurturing decision or self-compassionate gesture, every lovely moment of positive self-talk, each little laugh or tender moment we enjoy with ourselves, indeed through any loving act of self-care, we embrace ourselves and our lives. The daily joy of our own loving embrace is deeply nurturing and fortifying for our inner worlds. With thoughtful attention we can experience our lives as moving prayers of gratitude and respect for ourselves: celebrations of nature and aliveness. Living mindfully as prayers in motion, we may embody and express our thankfulness to be alive while exploring the tremendous depth of our innate creativity, strength and wisdom.

When we make time to be still, quiet and at one with ourselves, we become one with all there is. This felt experience of divine grace is love. Sufi mystic Rumi taught that the entire universe is within us; we need never feel alone. When we come home to ourselves we quite simply come home to love. At home within we can hear the wise, guiding calls of our spirits and sense vivid expressions of our intuition.

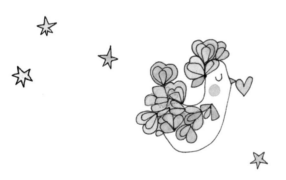

As we quieten down to connect with ourselves, we notice that our inner voice tends to whisper sacred messages to us, very gently. Spending time in our own sacred space within, we find, as timeless wisdom suggests, that the magical, subtle, enduring kingdom of love and life we seek is right here, within us.

*Enjoying our home within comes
with so many marvellous benefits, one
of which is that we naturally feel more
comfortable in all parts of our lives.*

Indeed, tending to our inner world allows us to move through our outer worlds feeling more peaceful and balanced each day. By caring for ourselves we also grow more content and resilient. We find ourselves responding to daily challenges rather than simply reacting to them. We notice that we feel more positive and energised, and more capable of positive decision making than ever before.

Truly awakening to the realisation that we have an inner home to which we may always retreat for constant refreshment, peace and inspiration is a profoundly fortifying and reassuring epiphany.

Dolly Parton once said that she could always close her eyes and go home, describing this as her greatest comfort. If we wish to enjoy our lives to the fullest we must create and nurture love at home within us by gifting ourselves our very own time and care. We must honour ourselves just as we are right now, while moving ever forward in the direction of our dreams. In doing so we create divine, spacious inner worlds in which we can truly relax and be ourselves: our own little mobile heavens. The more time we enjoy just being with ourselves lovingly, the more we realise and harness our innate ability to inspire and comfort ourselves at all times. In any moment we can simply close our eyes, place a hand on our heart, inhale deeply, and, upon exhalation, feel ourselves arriving back home within.

As we quieten down and connect with ourselves at home within we notice the wise, guiding calls of our spirits: sacred, whispers of our intuition.

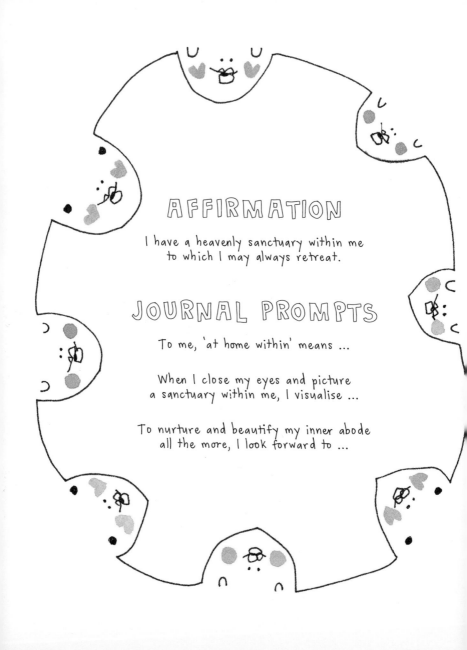

AFFIRMATION

I have a heavenly sanctuary within me
to which I may always retreat.

JOURNAL PROMPTS

To me, 'at home within' means ...

When I close my eyes and picture
a sanctuary within me, I visualise ...

To nurture and beautify my inner abode
all the more, I look forward to ...

PRAYER

Thank you life, for gifting me my heavenly home within. May I learn to take greater, more tender care of this sacred place with each new day. May my inner home be a generous, cosy place I can rest, relax and replenish my energy. May I receive wisdom in peace, at home within, as I deepen my trust in myself and in love. May my inner home be my most precious, sacred place of belonging and my constant, ever-giving source of comfort and joy.

THE GIFT
OF CHOOSING
OURSELVES

Choosing ourselves is essential self-care.
It means choosing to praise, soothe and compliment
ourselves rather than judge, stress or criticise.
It involves saying no when necessary and taking
slow, quiet moments to rest, relax and reflect.
Choosing ourselves invites us to explore our unique,
creative, heartfelt passions, both introspective
and adventurous, and to truly nourish our spirits.
Choosing ourselves every day through supportive
acts of self-care, especially through loving thoughts
and self-talk, is as natural and possible as it is
powerful and profound. It simply requires a little
bit of practice, and the pleasure of more time spent
nestled at home within.

Although it is a much-discussed tenet of emotional intelligence, many of us neglect to 'choose' ourselves. We are quite simply not on our own team! A great number of thoughts we think and actions we take each day distance us from ourselves. We might act lovingly towards others but harshly towards ourselves. We might speak kindly towards others yet dishonour and berate ourselves. We might have accidentally abandoned our home within and, as a result, feel out of sorts. When we feel out of sorts we might then blame ourselves, deepening our despair all the more. Yet we are so much greater and so much more magical than this. We can bring ourselves home with our own love and respect in any and every moment.

It can be easy to forget that we are the co-creators, not recipients, of our daily lives. Upon first glance it might seem that our circumstances are 'just the way they are', or simply ours by way of destiny or fate. This limited vision of our lives can make us feel hopeless, disenchanted and uninspired. We must acknowledge that we can 'choose' ourselves and our lives with every breath and step we take, harnessing our personal power and acknowledging how creative we truly are.

With each thought we choose to think, each act and word, we can love and approve of ourselves, quite simply manifesting more harmonious, fulfilling and love-filled lives for ourselves to savour. To choose ourselves and be on our own team is true self-empowerment. It is also a way of welcoming ourselves surely, safely back home into the comfort of our own wonderful love.

When we reclaim our personal
power and peace through self-care
we reclaim our joy.

When we choose ourselves, choose our bodies and choose our
lives, we grant ourselves permission to love and celebrate ourselves.
While we often seek approval from others with whom we share our
worlds, our own self-approval is the most fortifying, life-changing
love and acceptance we could ever receive. Experiencing our own
love means allowing limitless energy, fulfilment and deep healing
into our lives. The love we cultivate at home within becomes a
wellspring of energy from which we can endlessly draw strength
and comfort.

Self-care rituals are a wonderful approach to reinforcing and reminding ourselves of our own loving presence in daily life. Speaking or journaling our positive affirmations, taking a daily walk in a spirit of mindfulness, lighting a candle, saying a little prayer, expressing our gratitude, enjoying body care or nature therapy outdoors, making ourselves a nice cup of tea or simply taking time to breathe slowly and with loving attention are simple, unfussy self-care practices we can incorporate into our everyday lives. With a little time and care these simple rituals become daily markers of our commitment to choosing, loving and being there for ourselves.

Love is a vital, expansive energy;
a renewable resource available to us all.

Love is a vital, expansive energy, a renewable resource available
to us all. The only prerequisite for receiving and feeling love
is an open heart. In each moment of self-care, no matter how
small or simple, we choose ourselves and open our hearts to love.
Awakening to see self-care in this profound way stretches our hearts
and minds irreversibly beyond their old dimensions. In the divinity
of just a single moment we may acknowledge ourselves, sensing
and expressing the magnificent abundance of love and life that we
naturally possess. Let us feel supported, balanced and empowered by
our very own tender embrace at home within.

AFFIRMATION

I lovingly choose myself in
every moment.

JOURNAL PROMPTS

In my eyes, love is ...

In these ways, I care for myself ...

In these extra ways I commit to showing
myself even more love ...

PRAYER

With this prayer I give thanks for my active mind, my beautiful body and my soaring spirit. I am grateful for being gifted with greater insight and grace as I nurture myself more deeply. As I settle into my own love, may I embrace each day to care for myself through loving acts, words and thoughts. As I choose to support myself now, may the energy of life rise to elevate me all the more. May I sense unlimited joy and peace surrounding and uplifting me as I savour each day of my life.

SUBLIME
SURRENDER

There are many big and little ways we resist coming back home to our own love. While our sublime inner abode is ever ready and awaiting our presence, we might be too busy, distracted or too far afield, seeking to feel 'at home' anywhere else but within. Despite our various and elaborate defences, our love always grows stronger than our resistance through daily self-care. Little by little each of us can learn to come lovingly home to ourselves. Through cultivating resources in our personal self-care repertoire, we learn to navigate our resistance to accepting our own compassion and kindness. The truth is, we know love: we are an expression of it. We simply forget and need reminding that the most blissful homecoming is a return to our own love.

Although loving and approving of ourselves is simple, it isn't always easy. Indeed, it can be something that we even contest. Sadly, the material world around us often discourages us from choosing ourselves. Much of the media with which we interact today carries messages that suggest we are incomplete or in need of more. If we don't have our wits about us we too can buy into the idea that we are not ok, or not 'enough': that we are missing or lacking something. The time has come for us to outsmart what we see and hear, using our intuition and our discretion to transcend mindless comparison and live by higher ideals of self-care and compassion, kindness and courage.

We can unpack the gift
of choosing ourselves daily,
and watch our lives blossom.

Sometimes we might feel worried about spending time with
ourselves, at home within. Perhaps we haven't been home for
a while and worry about the state of our inner abode. Might unruly
feelings be spilling out of drawers? Might regrets be gathering dust
on bench-tops? Might wilting flowers in our untended inner garden
painfully signify our self-neglect … ? Our accumulated worries
might make us decide not to go home at all. It is safer, we think,
to just keep going. Keep busy. Keep moving. Keep living outwardly
and not truly, deeply within. It may be helpful to realise that such
resistance to home-coming is a collective experience. We share it.
We are not alone.

Despite what our fears may suggest, there is no safer, more wonderful place to be than at home within, in our own personal haven tucked cosily away from the outside world.

We can choose to renovate or restore our inner sanctuaries whenever we please – move things around, paint it afresh, arrange some flowers, light a candle – choose again, and choose ourselves. We are part of all that we have met in our lives. Our colourful, unique life stories make us who we are, each chapter and word bringing us to our present moment.

We can know ourselves completely and love ourselves. We can love ourselves just as we are right now, and as we grow and change into the future. There is nothing to fear and everything to gain when we return softly, gently home to our very own love.

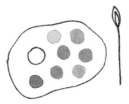

What is sure is that we all blossom and transform through love, not through disparagement. Noticing the density of our shame, blame, guilt and fear and actively transforming these energies through the lightness and peace of forgiveness, compassion and kindness is life-changing self-care. Each one of us deserves to experience our own unconditional love. Even if we don't know exactly how to forgive ourselves or others, simply by being compassionate and gentle with ourselves, we begin.

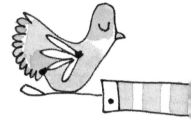

Our sheer willingness to move forward with love is enough
to catapult higher magic into action, usually in tremendously
powerful, albeit subtle, ways. We can watch ourselves flourish as we
open our hearts to the possibilities of healing and transformation.
Surrendering trustfully, we can allow life to love and support us as
we choose to love and support ourselves.

When we catch ourselves thinking unhelpful thoughts and intercept them, when we look in the mirror and smile at ourselves, when we receive criticism but immediately reassure ourselves that we are ok and that we did our very best, when we surround ourselves with people and things that reinforce our sense of self-worth, we come home.

When we don't know the answers or what to do next but are kind to ourselves all the same, we come home.

We must celebrate every small sparkle of progress we see and feel as we choose a kinder, more compassionate way of life with ourselves every day. Indeed, making a beautiful home within is a lifelong pleasure. A tremendous passion project and a magical, joyous, daily labour of love. We can all learn to navigate resistance to our own love, coming home in divine peace at last.

AFFIRMATION

It is safe for me to experience
the comfort of my own love.

JOURNAL PROMPTS

As I feel into the areas
of resistance in my
heart, I notice ...

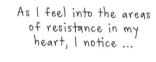

For me, cultivating deeper
self-respect would look
and feel like ...

When I am true to myself, I ...

PRAYER

From this day forward I choose to see myself through loving eyes. I find constant strength and inspiration to accept and adore myself, and I always celebrate my bravery and growth.

I choose to care for myself more deeply now, even in the moments I feel far from home. May peace blossom within me as I soothe, forgive and support myself at every turn. May lightness grace my heart so that I may feel and know the very best version of myself.

HONOURING OUR INNERMOST NEEDS

It takes courage to truly know, see and be ourselves; it takes self-compassion, faith and flexibility to nurture and nourish ourselves as we grow and change. Self-care is about meeting our physical, emotional and spiritual needs through our very own loving attention. Our needs really do matter, and they are worthy of our time and care. As we spend a little more time at home within day by day, we commit to honouring our ever-evolving selves. We sense our own truth and integrity, and come to know our own values and desires. As we draw greater strength, wisdom and inspiration within we find our lives aglow with the very energy and fulfilment, balance and peace we seek.

Many of us are taught with unwavering conviction to honour others' needs before our own. As a result many of us may find it much easier to gift our love, time and attention to others than to ourselves. Yet if we do not notice and take care of our own needs as a matter of priority, we cannot be safely equipped to cater to the needs of others. Soren Kierkegaard once wrote, 'It is easy to live for others, but we must live for ourselves'.

Living for ourselves through self-awareness and the practice of self-care allows us to cultivate energy for life so we can be of greater loving support not only to ourselves, but to those with whom we share our lives.

In this way noticing and meeting our own unique needs
is not selfish; it is the foundation of greater love.

While we all have needs we may find ourselves, for whatever
reason, not quite noticing them. We may have become so busy that
we have forgotten about ourselves. Perhaps our self-limiting habit
patterns and beliefs are clouding our vision, causing us to lose touch
with who we truly are and with the magnitude of our potential.
We might be neglecting to listen to the calls of our spirits and find
ourselves navigating outer worlds that, like mirrors of our worlds
within, fail to support or inspire us. Difficult feelings of guilt or
shame might be causing us to shut down or lock away very subtle,
sacred and foundational parts of ourselves, causing us deep hurt. In
all these ways, and many others, we can find our very important
personal needs being unseen and unmet.

It is perfectly reasonable to have needs of our own. We all require our basic, rudimentary needs to be met, such as our needs for food, water, love and shelter. Most of us also need touch, presence, kindness, beauty, inspiration, rest and relaxation, stimulating activities for our minds, bodies and spirits, and, very importantly, a sense of purpose – a raison d'être – a reason to awaken each morning and look forward to our day. Meaningful work has much to do with our sense of purpose; there is a sustaining energy of joy found in creativity, and in the deep satisfaction of receiving as we give.

Evidence of our unmet needs, while truly uncomfortable to see and feel, provides us with valuable insight. In our shared experiences of frustration and tiredness, despair, resentment or discontent, we receive inner wisdom encouraging us to take better notice of ourselves – to care for ourselves and acknowledge the areas of our lives requiring our mindful attention. Out of love and care for ourselves we can greet any uneasy sensation as a divine messenger from within: a direct, intuitive call to action.

'How can I love you more?'
'What is it that you need today?'

Simply quietening down and listening in, asking ourselves, 'How can I love you more?' or 'What is it that you need today?' are tremendous starting points. You may be surprised by the immediacy and strength of the comfort you receive in your awareness and grace. Indeed, self-care can work in both seen and unseen ways, with the most remarkable and magical benefits. Having the courage to attune ourselves to our own needs and desires while living in alignment with our values ignites our creativity, bringing our innermost dreams to life.

In order to enjoy the harmony, peace and balance we seek within and around us we must first acknowledge, honour and meet our own needs. We must accept the profound privilege and power that personal responsibility grants us and, without feeling needy or defensive, notice, accept and respect ourselves. We must welcome into the fullness and richness of our lives daily dialogue upon our innermost values and desires, thinking, speaking and acting from our hearts in truly courageous and authentic ways. Through our very own practice of self-care, the loving attention, acceptance and inspiration we seek naturally become our own personal gifts to enjoy.

AFFIRMATION

I notice my own unique needs
with loving attention.

JOURNAL PROMPTS

This is a list of my innermost needs ...

In these ways, I can honour my
innermost needs in daily life ...

What is it that I need today? ...

PRAYER

I am deeply thankful for my unique mind,
body and spirit. I honour my own needs
with joy, courage and compassion. May
loving awareness of my own uniqueness help
me to take tender care of myself, now and
always. May I be true to myself and stand
gracefully in my integrity, knowing myself,
respecting myself and loving myself more
each day of my life.

JUST AS
WE ARE

There could be nothing more comforting than
feeling soothed, safe and sound at home within.
We feel happier, healthier, more resilient and more
balanced when we design our lives in support of
our own unique natures; when we truly know and
care for ourselves as the one-off creations we
miraculously are. Introverted and sensitive people
will require different self-care to those more
extroverted and outgoing. Quiet time will be a
healing elixir for some, while for others enjoying
dynamic activities will be most restorative. To love
ourselves is to know and honour ourselves as we
truly are, and to nurture ourselves in comfort and
confidence as we learn, change and grow.

Respecting our uniqueness is essential self-care. It is much easier to honour our unique selves when we spend quality time within, sensing our personal needs and values and allowing ourselves to freely explore our dreams, instincts and aspirations. When we truly meet ourselves we begin to sense our very own energy and nature, observing that our daily self-care needs are completely unique to our personalities, moods and spirits. We also see that our needs shift and change as we do over time, making our life stories deeply satisfying adventures of self-discovery.

When we spend more time at home within, we find it harder to be anything other than our authentic selves. We become anchored so deeply within our own love and acceptance that we no longer need to seek approval from others to feel safe and loveable. We needn't exhaust ourselves playing outwardly bigger, better, bolder or brighter versions of ourselves for others, nor bend over backwards to be acceptable to others. Our worth is innate; it is not something that we need to prove or earn. By practising self-care we flourish in self-love and self-respect.

We learn to feel safe, soothed
and sound, just as we are.
We learn to enjoy ourselves
and really, truly live.

As simple as it sounds, we can forget that we can be our authentic selves and be loved and loveable. We do not need to be anything more or less than ourselves. We are by nature whole and complete. We are dignified as we are, and we are worthy of being seen, appreciated, loved and understood. Those in our lives who love us for something we aren't, or aren't able to give, will naturally fall away when we grow to live freely in our integrity and truth. Those who really love us will remain, loving us still, celebrating and supporting us as we support and celebrate them.

These days the majority of our stress is interpersonal, derived from the way we experience ourselves in relationship to others. We experience tension when we are untrue to ourselves – when we become what we think we should be. In contrast, relaxation and bliss alight upon us when we embrace and embody who we truly are.

We no longer need to frighten or diminish ourselves with our own unkind, unhelpful thoughts. We can intercept old, outworn habit patterns and behaviours, turning the tide with our very own love.

We may need to make changes in order to embrace and honour ourselves in daily life. Even if the changes we make are very small, we can make them steadily. We can commit to knowing and caring for ourselves more deeply each day, and allowing our inner voice to be the kindest voice we know. We can honour ourselves and, irrespective of our circumstances, come home to ourselves moment to moment with unwavering, unconditional love.

While the people with whom
we share our worlds naturally
influence, inspire and affect our
paths, we cannot forget that our
lives are ours to create and enjoy.

It is essential that we sense and respect our own personal energy, values and needs so that we do not unwittingly merge into the stories, expectations or wishes of others. Being individual of spirit is our tremendous privilege and gift.

Nobody else can think our thoughts for us, nor access our luminous, private haven within. Indeed, our hearts are uniquely ours with which to sense and feel, our spirits our own divine energy to nurture, express and enjoy. We are entitled to have unique needs, and our needs are allowed to shift and change over time, as they naturally do. We are allowed to take time to know and care for ourselves lovingly over the entire course of our lives. In doing so we can always feel comfortable and safe at home within, even amidst great change and profound personal growth. Herein lies the beauty of self-care as a truly transformative, magical manifestation of our very own love.

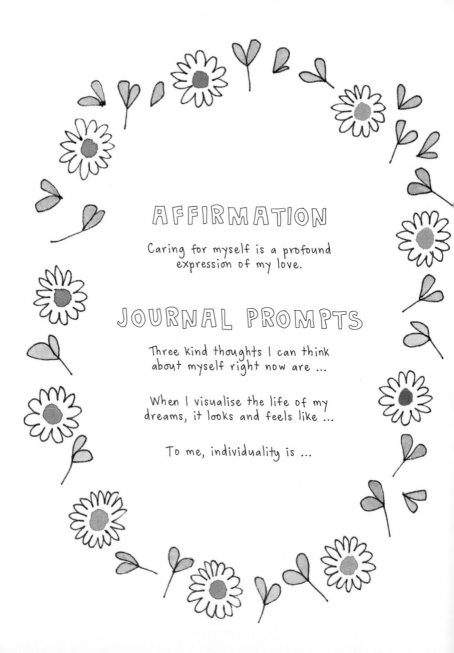

AFFIRMATION

Caring for myself is a profound
expression of my love.

JOURNAL PROMPTS

Three kind thoughts I can think
about myself right now are ...

When I visualise the life of my
dreams, it looks and feels like ...

To me, individuality is ...

PRAYER

I am grateful for the gift of my individuality, and for the innate wisdom and creativity I possess to make positive changes in my life. I know that I am worthy of my own time and care, and I blossom in the embrace of my own love. I accept and approve of myself just as I am right now, and celebrate my life as I move forward in the direction of my dreams.

THE JOY
OF NEW
BEGINNINGS

Buddha reminds us that each morning we are born again. What we do today matters most. The art of self-care invites us to nurture an intimate relationship with ourselves and, regardless of how we might have been or might be right now, continue to grow, blossom and move forward more lovingly each day. Through each act of self-care we strengthen and nourish ourselves. We find our wellbeing flourishing, our delight expanding, our resilience building and our satisfaction heartfelt.

The joy of self-care offers us endless new beginnings: limitless fresh chances to love and respect ourselves.

When we begin taking greater care of ourselves we very soon notice that little things are big things. A kind word to ourselves can change our day. Enjoying a bath or taking a walk in nature can lift our spirits. Reaching out to loved ones and new friends is a balm for our hearts, and the bunch of flowers we gifted ourselves today will bring us daily delight for a whole new week. The beauty of practising small, simple rituals of self-care to cater to our 'littler' daily needs and desires is that these small acts of love culminate to help us meet our 'bigger', innermost needs over time.

We cannot underestimate the power of
a single divine minute of rest, reflection
or grace to elevate and refresh us.

When we are truly loving and present with ourselves, even very small pockets of time and space, or very small moments of self-kindness and compassion, can become immensely healing resets and powerful new beginnings. One deep breath. One smile. One positive thought. One blissful moment of gratitude.

Self-care is a pleasure to practise and enjoy, as it involves doing and experiencing more of what we truly love, incorporating nurturing practices and rituals into our daily lives. As we lovingly nurture and attend to our home within we become the recipients of our very own intuitive wisdom and guidance. We notice the stirring in our hearts when we feel happy and at peace.

We sense the essence of comfort and joy when in the presence of those with whom we are free to be ourselves. We pick up little cues when we need to retreat or protect ourselves, slow down, reconsider, or take a little more time with our own thoughts and feelings. Indeed, by connecting with ourselves we connect with our unique and invaluable inner guidance system: our intuition.

Taking more notice of our subtle selves through nurturing self-care, we notice that thoughts and feelings, signs and symbols, even physical sensations such as butterflies in our tummies, are delivering messages within us. Attuning ourselves to our inner wisdom supports us to take initiative as we care for ourselves in daily life. Paying compassionate attention to our minds and bodies each day strengthens our intuitive wisdom, and deepens our experience of self-love. Each gentle moment we take with ourselves, to know and care for ourselves, is a new beginning in the way of self-love. The freshness of such love is magical, uncomplicated and unlimited.

The time it takes to enjoy
self-care is ours to make.

When we enjoy a positive relationship with time there is always enough for us, always time for self-care and new beginnings. Conversely, with a hurried, untrusting relationship with time, we never seem to have enough. We can allow time to work for us by actively cultivating a positive relationship with it, and letting it bedazzle us with its generosity. Each moment we gift ourselves in the name of self-care imbues us with greater energy to go about our lives, just as a rested field yields a bountiful crop. It is a joy to realise that the pleasure of self-care can have such practical benefits, and make such complete sense.

It is never too late to love and care for ourselves. Irrespective of our past and present stories we can always choose ourselves, and open our hearts and minds to the practice of self-care. We can practise a bolstering little prayer for instant comfort, or quite simply take a few slow, deep breaths to welcome ourselves back home within. In moments in which it seems difficult to meet our needs straight away we can comfort ourselves, tenderly reassuring ourselves, 'I promise to take care of you', while actively planning our next, most mindful, positive step forward.

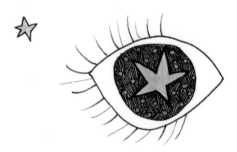

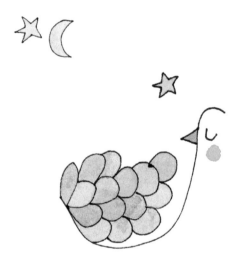

It is empowering to realise that we can always turn to ourselves, instantly and lovingly, to create a new beginning. We can always soothe ourselves and be there for ourselves completely, no matter what may come. Yes. Our own loving care is so soothing and nourishing, so rich and life-changing.

AFFIRMATION

I am ready and willing to experience
joy with every new beginning.

JOURNAL PROMPTS

Little things that always help bring
me back to centre include ...

In these ways, I could make time
for extra self-care ...

I see this moment as a new
beginning for me to ...

PRAYER

Thank you, life, for the endless new beginnings you grant me to be myself. To be brave and true, to love and trust myself all the more, to try again, to see differently, and to change for the better. Each time I see myself growing and changing, I acknowledge my efforts and my magnificence. In the bliss of my own unconditional love, I find clarity and strength.

LOVING FOUNDATIONS FOR RADIANT WELLBEING

+ Self-Care Inspirations Checklist

Radiant wellbeing arises from a mind, body and spirit humming together in harmony. When we practise self-care we naturally make more compassionate, thoughtful and positive choices in daily life. We cultivate kindness and gratitude, nourish our whole selves, nurture our beauty and commune with nature. We value deep rest, structure healthy personal boundaries, express our innate creativity and move our bodies with joy. Wellbeing is not a part of life but a way of life built upon uplifting daily self-care rituals that inspire, comfort and elevate us.

Loving kindness

A kind inner voice is the very best therapist, beautician, life coach and friend we could ever wish for. We can always choose to think kind thoughts, speak kind words and perform kind acts to nurture a loving world within and around us. Kindness towards ourselves allows us to move through each day feeling lighter, more peaceful and more confident, easing our path and imbuing us with grace. As we practise kindness as self-care it naturally becomes easier to be more generous, tender and patient with others, enhancing and transforming all our relationships. Happy and healthy relationships contribute greatly to our wellbeing, bolstering our vitality and joy.

Gratitude in the moment

Being present and open to all the riches we possess in a spirit of gratitude can in an instant transform our experience of life. The simplest things we can take for granted may be another person's longing: sunshine on our skin, the sound of rain, the ability to see, or the luxury of the creature comforts we savour at home. Attuning ourselves to the fortifying energy of gratitude as part of our self-care practice allows us to experience the abundance of life. Gratitude inspires us to not squander another moment estranged from our happiness, but rather to live, fully. Keep a gratitude journal. Say thank you. Notice and celebrate beautiful moments, and actively count your blessings. Let the uplifting energy of gratitude elevate your wellness and bring you peace.

Embracing beauty

Our true beauty shines from within and is a celebration of our individuality and authenticity. Radiant beauty sparkles as an attitude to life: one of wonder, courage and faith. Early nights, quiet moments, laughs with friends, adventures in nature, nourishing food and joyous movement are just some of the most beautifying elixirs available to us. It is essential to notice and treasure our own unique beauty, the unique beauty of others and the spellbinding beauty of our earth. As we care for ourselves with love each day, we can broaden any limiting concepts we harbour about beauty, and free ourselves to embrace ourselves and embrace life.

Savouring rest

When we rest and relax we restore our energy, powering ourselves to live vibrant and creative lives. It is a joy to comfort and nurture ourselves, to indulge our senses and luxuriate in stillness and peace. Giving ourselves permission to slow down and let go every day is essential self-care. We might curl up on the sofa with a good book, a pet or a beautiful view. Enjoy a mindfulness meditation or some soothing rounds of slow, deep breathing. We might savour a majestic sunrise or say a little prayer under the stars. Cultivating regular sleeping rhythms encourages deeper, more restful sleep. Soothing bedtime rituals, from journaling to gently stretching, listening to calming music or sipping a relaxing herbal tea, can help us to feel nurtured and settled as we prepare to welcome sleep. When we regularly celebrate slow, quiet and blissful moments with ourselves we find ourselves unwinding, resetting and returning home within with far greater ease.

Nourishing our bodies

Thriving in our physical bodies is best achieved with high-vibrational edible nourishment, ample water and joyous activity. As vessels for our spirits, our physical bodies are very sacred parts of ourselves to be nurtured and nourished with care. When we eat a rainbow of real, whole foods in a plant rich diet inspired by nature, we nourish ourselves at a cellular level. This means we are supporting our bodies to function at their very best. Healthy home cooking is a joy to explore and must not be underestimated as a profound and powerful act of self-care. Caring about the origins of our food, and preparing and savouring our food with pleasure and gratitude, ensures that we fortify ourselves not only with vitamins and minerals but with the potent energy of love.

Joyous movement

As we deeply nourish our bodies we experience vitality to enjoy the movement for which we were so beautifully designed. As we move our bodies freely in diverse ways that we truly enjoy, we experience a heightened sense of fluidity, spaciousness and wellbeing. We energise our spirits to feel buoyant, fresh, flexible and alive. We can walk, dance, swim, practise yoga or learn the trapeze if we please ... the list of activities we can enjoy is endless! Move in your own way, and be intuitive with your body. Tune into your body's language, and explore its shifting needs with love.

Loving boundaries

Nurturing healthy boundaries is a crucial yet little discussed and commonly misunderstood form of self-care. When we respect ourselves we are generous of spirit without overextending ourselves to others at our own expense. We nurture and maintain personal boundaries to assist us as we support our own vitality, energy and peace. We can do all we do in life with love and care and allow others to do the same. We can give and receive with joy as part of the flow of life, always ensuring that we care for ourselves while offering genuine, loving attention to others in ways with which we feel confident and comfortable. Setting personal boundaries is not unkind; it is essential. It involves saying no when needed, enjoying the company of loving, supportive people, and expressing our true feelings with honesty and tact. It also involves being mindful and discerning with our time each day so as to create a healthy balance between work, rest and play.

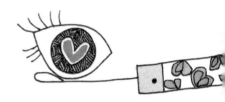

Enjoying our home in nature

Communing with nature is ancient wisdom's timeless answer to self-care. When we connect with nature, we connect with ourselves: as expressions of life we are part of nature. We inherently understand her ways, and with a little time, care and intention we can learn to harmonise with her rhythms. Immersing ourselves in the natural world we gain perspective as we experience beauty, awe and gratitude. We learn patience and resilience observing natural law, and feel the magic of moment to moment miracles unfolding before our eyes. We might observe a shooting star or see a butterfly emerge from a chrysalis, watch a bud blossom into a rose or spot bedazzling cloud formations taking shape in the sky. Communing with nature we come home. We experience our remarkable place as living, breathing beings in an interconnected, inspirational web of life.

Attuning to our spirits

Listening to our inner voice is critical for our wellness. We are multi-sensory beings with the faculty of intuition our guiding star within. If we ignore the calls of our spirits we damage and degrade our health. We diminish our vital energy. As our health is energetic, it is essential that we look after the health of our spirits by nurturing our inner worlds, making time and space to connect with our own healing energy and paying credence to the profound guiding wisdom within us.

Breathe

Our breath is a gift that we too often take for granted. It is our life force and the language of our spirit. When we slow and deepen our breathing we calm and clear our minds. We notice that our minds follow our breath, and that we can learn to soothe ourselves simply through tending to our breathing with love, patience, energy and care. The art of breath awareness is mindfulness in action, bringing us promptly back into the present moment: the moment in which all magic and transformation happens; the only moment we have. The past is gone and our future is not guaranteed. We must breathe our breath of life, right now. For more on breathing, turn to page 131.

It is essential to remember that self-care does not involve punishing regimes or deprivation. True self-care is a celebration of our aliveness. With our own loving kindness, creativity and care, we can joyously enhance our vitality in daily life. We can support ourselves to feel alive and truly at home within, experiencing radiant energy and resounding inner peace. Through the practice of self-care, as we honour, respect and love ourselves, we naturally embody true, vibrant wellness.

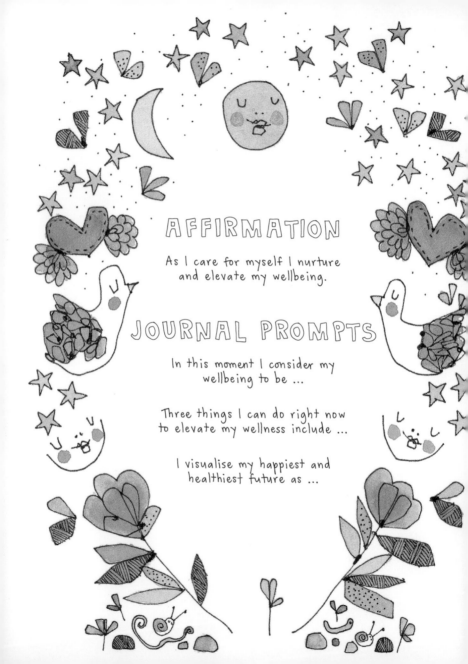

AFFIRMATION

As I care for myself I nurture
and elevate my wellbeing.

JOURNAL PROMPTS

In this moment I consider my
wellbeing to be ...

Three things I can do right now
to elevate my wellness include ...

I visualise my happiest and
healthiest future as ...

PRAYER

I look forward to taking care of my mind,
body and spirit each day as I bring my
loving attention, time and care to all parts of
my life. I am grateful for the harmony I feel
within and around me when I love and care
for myself. I choose to notice the abundance
of joy and inspiration surrounding me each
day as I embrace wellbeing as my way of
life. I ask for extra strength and motivation
now as I commit to myself, and I promise to
celebrate every little sign of my progress.

SELF-CARE INSPIRATIONS CHECKLIST

- [ ] Choose positive self-talk
- [ ] Choose self-kindness
- [ ] Enjoy early nights
- [ ] Make soothing bedtime rituals
- [ ] Earthing – walking barefoot upon the earth
- [ ] Choose joy, because I can!
- [ ] Practise gratitude to refresh my perspective
- [ ] Commit to self-compassion
- [ ] Eat real food for vibrant, radiant wellness
- [ ] Enjoy therapeutic herbal teas
- [ ] Present myself with love and care
- [ ] Select natural beauty and body care
- [ ] Drink ample fresh water each day
- [ ] Cultivate a regular, supportive sleep cycle
- [ ] Intercept and interrupt any unhelpful thoughts
- [ ] Surround myself with positive people who appreciate me
- [ ] Nurture healthy boundaries for my wellbeing and happiness
- [ ] Learn to say no with grace and confidence

- [ ] Honour my uniqueness with thankfulness and respect
- [ ] Craft and enjoy my very own unique style of being
- [ ] Seek support whenever I need it
- [ ] Give myself real compliments (and accept them!)
- [ ] Journal for self-healing and self-expression
- [ ] Explore essential oils, crystals and natural remedies
- [ ] Express and explore my innate creativity
- [ ] Cultivate courage with my thoughts, words and actions
- [ ] Nurture my home environment as a beautiful sanctuary
- [ ] Celebrate my body with joyous movement
- [ ] Explore my intuition; my inner wisdom
- [ ] Stargaze, moongaze
- [ ] Savour sunrises and sunsets
- [ ] Enjoy decadent scented baths
- [ ] Wrap myself in cosy pyjamas and comfy clothes
- [ ] Call my loved ones for heartfelt conversations
- [ ] Savour little siestas
- [ ] Value my vulnerability and be true to myself
- [ ] Make quiet time for meditation and prayer
- [ ] Close my eyes and tune into my breath
- [ ] Celebrate self-care as my way of life

SELF-CARE AND CHANGING THE WORLD

Caring for ourselves truly is living by example.
Words are not even required when we live in a
spirit of self-love, acceptance and approval, as our
radiant energy speaks for itself, inviting others to
love and know themselves more deeply too. To truly
care for ourselves is to choose an uplifting, creative
and revolutionary way of life, one that creates a
ripple effect of joy, peace and healing wherever
we go. As we honour ourselves, we encourage and
inspire others to do the same. And as we come to see
and love ourselves, we may truly see and love those
with whom we share life.

The art of self-care begins with us – but it is a conversation, a kind of magic in motion, that extends well beyond ourselves. Caring for ourselves shifts our personal energy. When we care for ourselves, everything – the way we carry ourselves, the way we speak of and approve of ourselves – is a living, breathing example of love. We are light and gentle with ourselves. We praise and compliment ourselves without fear or shame. We bring immense joy to ourselves and others as we freely share our gifts in daily life, carrying with us an emanating sense of ease, grace and inner peace.

As human beings we gravitate towards love.
We are compelled by love.

By nature love comforts us, sparks our curiosity, piques our interest and warms our hearts. Whether we realise it or not, our own self-care and self-love positively and profoundly affect all others in our orbit. It is in these very subtle, peaceful and gentle ways that we truly can change the world.

We all learn by observation and osmosis. We can learn the way children do, observing, remembering and repeating; not necessarily being directly taught particular things with focused energy and action but learning simply by absorbing energy. What if we were to be honest with ourselves and one another? Wear no masks, offer no performances, and simply come as we are. What a different world this would be.

We could be vulnerable and courageous, vivid and authentic, curious, confused, brimming with wonder … all parts of us fully alive and integrated into a completely loveable, loved and accepted whole. We could still understand the value of discretion and appropriateness but be ourselves fearlessly, without any withholding. We could naturally celebrate ourselves and one another. We could, and we can.

It is only when we truly see and meet ourselves that we may, with great compassion, see our own same love, fear, joy and sorrow in those with whom we share our lives. Honouring our own needs, we grow in respect not only for ourselves but also for all other human beings. We can offer ourselves respect and spaciousness to enjoy and be ourselves fully and, in doing so, encourage others to explore, nurture and express their own needs too. In this way we can support each other into healing and happiness, understanding that when we change, the world around us changes.

Self-soothing through self-care is a valuable art. It is a skill that spending more time at home within supports us to master in daily life. While soothing ourselves with kind, compassionate self-talk, uplifting thoughts and meaningful acts of self-care is absolutely essential for our health and wellness, we were not created to be separate from one another. Indeed, life was made for sharing. We must trust in the solidity of ourselves and the completeness of our home within, but know all the same that we are not navigating this life alone. That we can always reach out and connect. That we are made of the same cloth, and that shared threads eternally unite us.

Seeking support when needed
is self-care wisdom.

When talking honestly to friends, family and wellbeing professionals of our choosing we come to find that deep concerns we may privately face – concerns that can bring us immense pain and make us feel very alone – are very much shared, lived parts of our human experience. Spending just a few minutes in sincere conversation with another human being, we touch upon common ground – ground that we can traverse together in generosity of truth and spirit. Inviting compassionate, trusted support into our lives is both courageous and wise. Acknowledging that we can't always do things alone, that we are allowed to require support, and that we are all divine works in progress is true, loving self-care in action.

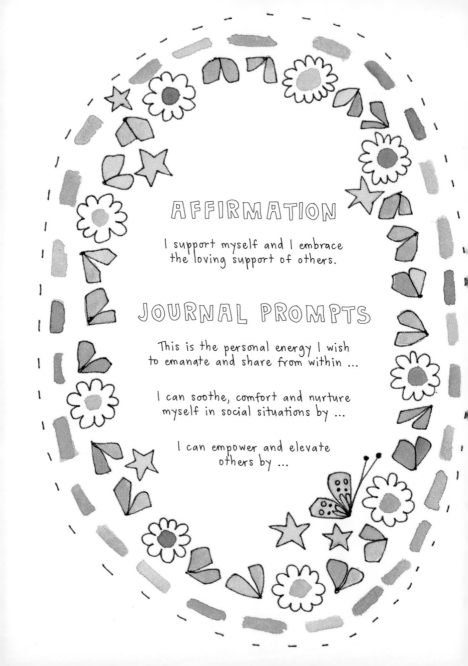

AFFIRMATION

I support myself and I embrace
the loving support of others.

JOURNAL PROMPTS

This is the personal energy I wish
to emanate and share from within ...

I can soothe, comfort and nurture
myself in social situations by ...

I can empower and elevate
others by ...

PRAYER

With this prayer I give thanks for my life.
I am grateful to see that connecting with
others allows me to feel and understand what
it truly means to be human. May I awaken
more fully each day to the peace and power
within my heart. May strength grace me as I
change the world with kind words, courageous
actions and loving thoughts. May I feel more
at home within myself each day, and may the
generous care and tenderness that I receive
from others nourish my spirit.

SELF-CARE
AND MAGICAL
ENERGY

We are just as much heavenly as we are human.
The material, physical world as we see and know it
constitutes only a very, very small part of reality.
We are energetic beings in a world of energy, and
we are part of so much more than we could ever
see or know. In a spirit of wonder and gratitude for
our miraculousness, we may feel deeply, consistently
encouraged to care for ourselves in ways that
nourish and nurture the vitality of our spirits. We
all have an innate ability to access and harness
magical energy, wisdom and healing within ourselves.
While the following suggestions, which touch on
visualisation and working with energy, may seem
a little abstract at first, I encourage you to explore
them. They are simple, powerful self-care techniques
that can gift us the clarity, protection, strength
and peace we seek.

Breath awareness

One very simple, swift and transformative way we can self-regulate our biology, soothing, settling and refreshing ourselves, is through mindful breathing. Bringing our awareness to our breath, breathing deeply in and then breathing slowly, fully out with a thorough, satisfying exhale, returns us right back to centre: back to our present moment and back into our bodies. We are often so busy that we lose a sense of connection between our minds and bodies in real time. Being aware of and attentive to our breath quite simply reestablishes and nourishes this precious connection.

Deep breathing is a tonic for our nervous systems. It decelerates our stress responses and sends healing, relaxing signals to every muscle, organ and cell in our bodies. Oxygenating our cells and really 'breathing' into our bodies helps us to function beautifully, just as we were designed to do. By routinely elongating our in- and out-breaths in a smooth and even rhythm we can learn to relax and let go, changing our biology and our lives. Paying attention to the spaces in between our breaths can help us to become all the more present, and all the more enchanted by our breath.

I like to lie down in a comfortable position, close my eyes and place my hands upon my belly. I then breathe slowly in, right to the very top of my lungs upon my inhale, then deeply, fully out, from down in my belly upon each exhale. I feel my hands rise and fall in a lovely rhythm. I count slowly, breathing in to ten, then out to ten. Experiment with your own timing to see what feels right for you.

Make sure you never feel dizzy or light-headed when working with your breath – it should feel comfortable and relaxing. Play some beautiful, gentle music if you please. I consider rounds of deep breathing to be 'breath meditation', and it is possible for each and every one of us to experience this lifelong gift and pleasure for ourselves. Breathe, and radically enhance your daily self-care practice.

Healing body scan

We can create powerful healing for our bodies with our very own loving attention. Gently tune into your heartbeat and the flow of your breath. What other subtle sensations can you feel within your body? Do you feel heat or cold, movement or tingling? If you sense any discomfort or pain, rather than direct frustration or angst to these hurting parts of you, send your love there now. Imagine soothing and relaxing any tight or stressed areas of your body with your loving awareness and with the gentle spaciousness of your breath. Enjoy a little time each day to harness and grow your very own healing energy.

Heart space

You might like to try this exercise at home within. As you inhale, imagine your in-breath circulating, clearing and opening your heart with new, fresh energy. Inhale as if breathing into your heart. Make space within and around your heart with each new breath. Gently placing your hand or a little finger upon your heart can help you to feel the living, breathing life force of love that is always active there, dwelling inside you. Open your heart to yourself. With each breath, be open to the love within you and ask it to illuminate and shape your path forward. In Greek philosophical tradition the word 'nous' refers to the 'spiritual eye' of the heart. By acquainting ourselves with our inner worlds we can learn to 'see' not just with our eyes but with our hearts. As we breathe new life into our heart's vision, we breathe new life into ourselves.

Protecting and nurturing our energy

Each day we encounter the personal energy of those with whom we share our lives: friends, family, colleagues, even strangers. In addition to this we are constantly interacting with the energy of the places and spaces we visit and occupy. Being mindful of the energy we feel within and around us as we navigate our daily lives is self-care. There are many ways we can nurture and protect our personal energy to strengthen our wellbeing. Crystals and essential oils can cleanse, fortify and uplift us. You might like to explore clear and rose quartz, black tourmaline, obsidian and jasper for vitality and energetic protection. Pure essential oils of lavender, frankincense, lemon, grapefruit and cypress are all wonderful options for supporting positive energy and wellness. Burning dried sage or Palo Santo, a sweet aromatic 'holy' wood, are traditional botanical cleansing methods that help to clear our inner and outer spaces. Prayers, meditations and visualisations like the ones found in these pages work beautifully too. May the simple energetic techniques that follow bring you inspiration, nourishment and support.

⭐ Sit back in your heart. Visualise a beautiful, cosy armchair in your heart into which you can settle back at any moment. In this way, rather than wearing your proverbial 'heart on your sleeve', you can be present to others with true care and compassion while keeping vital energy for yourself. You needn't love and support others at your own expense. You can sit back, relax, and take care of yourself while still taking very good, loving care of others.

⭐ Arm's length. There are times we need distance from others. Protecting our energetic space supports our wellness and peace. Nobody can enter our energetic field unless we allow them to. This may sound esoteric, but it is true: we are always in control. At any moment, visualise yourself in a beautiful white 'egg' of energy — a luminous, protective, energetic bubble. This might extend an arm's length around you, and even more, if you wish. Let your focused intention and the energy of your mind bedazzle you as you explore this profoundly empowering resource.

⭐ Forehead and tailbone. In the process of evolution we lost our tails, yet we still have our tailbones! Energetically this vulnerable little part of our bodies can be a common holding place for fear. Place one hand across your tailbone and the other across your forehead, over your 'third eye' or pineal gland. This simple gesture alone can immediately restore a sense of comfort and safety within, especially when partnered with a few nice, slow, deep breaths. Pause here, close your eyes, and enjoy the comfort and power of your very own healing energy.

⭐ Dive in and out of a golden pool. When exiting an awkward or stressful exchange we needn't marinate in negative thoughts or bad energy. Visualise a beautiful golden pool and dive into it. As you emerge, feel yourself utterly cleansed and fortified. Proceed with your day.

Receiving divine assistance

Whenever we desire, we can humbly ask for divine assistance through our prayers and meditations. These needn't be fussy, formal or intellectual requests for grace – they can be very short and simple. Pausing and genuinely asking to be filled with grace at any moment in time, we can suddenly feel ourselves imbued with divine energy. We become recipients of serendipitous, perfectly timed guidance as we move forward, learning to surrender, live fully and lovingly, and watch our needs being met in magical, often unpredictably perfect ways.

We can invite freshness, positivity and vitality into our lives moment to moment by elevating our personal energy to commune with higher possibilities. This means sculpting our reality by fine-tuning the quality of our thoughts and the worlds we create: the people, places, media, food, music, art, words and various inspirations with which we nourish ourselves in daily life. With divine assistance, and in the sacred moments we create with ourselves, we can release our grip on patterns and ideas that have held us back.

As we unblock, free and forgive ourselves, we allow greater goodness, peace and joy to embrace us. In this open, expansive state of human-being we can enjoy more expression, more compassion, more feeling and more richness in our lives. We can learn to create and enjoy our very own versions of heaven on earth in which we lovingly care for ourselves, each other and our earth, in which we dwell gracefully, truly at home within.

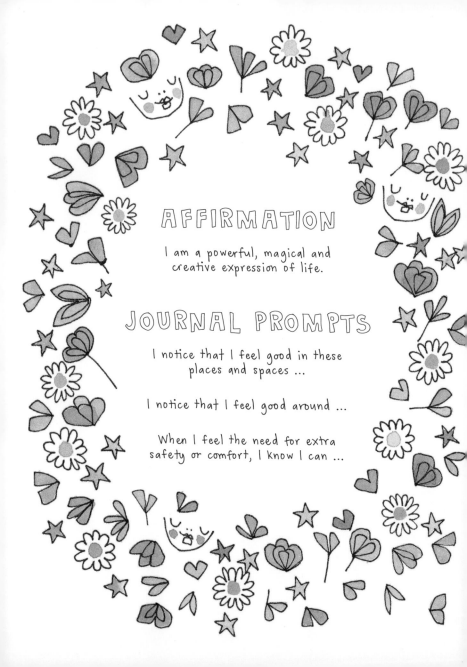

AFFIRMATION

I am a powerful, magical and creative expression of life.

JOURNAL PROMPTS

I notice that I feel good in these places and spaces ...

I notice that I feel good around ...

When I feel the need for extra safety or comfort, I know I can ...

PRAYER

With this prayer I express gratitude for my very own healing and creative powers. I know that I am the recipient of great magic and miracles, and I commit to opening my eyes to the richness of life. I support myself to feel safe, soothed and uplifted each day, deepening my awareness of the world of energy. I freely explore the power of self-care, inviting peace and joy to elevate and inspire me more each day. With true grace and faith, I create my experience of heaven on earth.

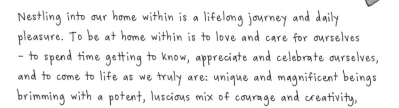

Nestling into our home within is a lifelong journey and daily pleasure. To be at home within is to love and care for ourselves — to spend time getting to know, appreciate and celebrate ourselves, and to come to life as we truly are: unique and magnificent beings brimming with a potent, luscious mix of courage and creativity, vulnerability and openness and zest.

As we embrace the richness of our lives and ourselves we cultivate true, sustainable wellbeing. With brave and open hearts we may transcend any limitations holding us back and blossom resplendently in confidence, faith and bliss. Indeed, in the garden of our own grace, all aspects of our truest nature may express themselves and flourish. With generosity of spirit, gratitude and kindness, and in the safety of our own unconditional love, there is no situation we cannot navigate.

We must choose ourselves — forgive ourselves, love, support and enjoy ourselves — each day of our lives. We must choose to keep our thoughts and inner voice in loving check, and devote energy to self-care. In doing so we harness true vitality to share our gifts with the world. As we venture outward on journeys of all kinds we may know that, no matter where we may roam, we are always and effortlessly at home within. As part of the circle of life, as figments of the greatest miracle of creation, we have the light of life ever aglow within us: a little lantern forever guiding us home.

ACKNOWLEDGEMENTS

This book came together like a dream. I would like to thank all the wonderful people involved behind the scenes for their time and care. I am grateful for the wonderful team at Hardie Grant Books in Melbourne for their faith in me and their dedication to my words and pictures. Thank you to Sandy Grant, Pam Brewster, Kirstie Grant, Jane Grant, Todd Rechner and the lovely Mietta Yans, with whom I worked on the design of this book. Thank you to Meaghan Thomson for assisting me with graphic design elements, and to Mick Smith and his team at Splitting Image for so carefully digitally converting my original artworks for print. I would like to express appreciation for my editor Allison Hiew, whose gentle approach allows my words to come to you so truly and naturally. Thank you to my loving network of family and friends for their tremendous and constant support, and thank you, dear reader, for welcoming this book into your heart and world. My greatest gift is knowing it may bring you precious moments of peace, joy and inspiration on your lifelong journey home.

Love, Meredith X

Published in 2020 by Hardie Grant Books,
an imprint of Hardie Grant Publishing

Hardie Grant Books (Melbourne)
Building 1, 658 Church Street
Richmond, Victoria 3121

Hardie Grant Books (London)
5th & 6th Floors
52-54 Southwark Street
London SE1 1UN

hardiegrantbooks.com

All rights reserved. No part of this publication may be reproduced, stored in a retrieval system or
transmitted in any form by any means, electronic, mechanical, photocopying, recording or otherwise,
without the prior written permission of the publishers and copyright holders.

The moral rights of the author have been asserted.

Copyright © Meredith Gaston 2020

At Home Within
ISBN 978 1 74379 688 7

10 9 8 7 6 5 4 3 2 1

A catalogue record for this
book is available from the
National Library of Australia

Publisher: Pam Brewster
Editor: Allison Hiew
Designer: Mietta Yans
Production Manager: Todd Rechner

Colour reproduction by Splitting Image Colour Studio
Printed in China by Leo Paper Products LTD.

MIX
Paper from
responsible sources
FSC® C020056

The paper this book is printed on is from FSC®-certified
forests and other sources. FSC® promotes environmentally
responsible, socially beneficial and economically viable
management of the world's forests.